MRJC
6/15

Stay, Kay!

by Marie Powell

illustrated by Amy Cartwright

Ideas for Parents and Teachers

Amicus Readers let children practice reading at early reading levels. Familiar words and concepts with close illustration-text matches support early readers.

Before Reading

- Discuss the cover illustration with the child. What does it tell him?
- Ask the child to predict what she will learn in the book.

Read the Book

- "Walk" through the book and look at the illustrations. Let the child ask questions.
- Point out the colored words. Ask the child what is the same about them (spelling, ending sound).
- Read the book to the child, or have the child read to you.

After Reading

- Use the word family list at the end of the book to review the text.
- Prompt the child to make connections. Ask: *What other words end with -ay?*

Amicus Readers are published by Amicus
P.O. Box 1329, Mankato, MN 56002
www.amicuspublishing.us

Library of Congress Cataloging-in-Publication Data
Powell, Marie, 1958-
  Stay, Kay! / Marie Powell.
    pages cm. -- (Word families)
  K to Grade 3.
  Audience: Age 6
  ISBN 978-1-60753-585-0 (hardcover) --
  ISBN 978-1-60753-651-2 (pdf ebook)
1. Reading--Phonetic method. 2. Readers (Primary) I. Title.
LB1573.3.P697 2014
372.46'5--dc23
                      2013043983

Illustrations by Amy Cartwright

Produced for Amicus by The Peterson Publishing Company and Red Line Editorial.

Editor Jenna Gleisner
Designer Craig Hinton
Printed in the United States of America
Mankato, MN
9-2014
PO1228
10 9 8 7 6 5 4 3 2

Today I am meeting my friend Kay at the park.

It is a cloudy **day**.
"Those clouds look **gray**,"
says **Kay**.
"Let's swing **anyway**!"
I **say**.

Tiny raindrops fall.

"I don't want to play

anymore," says Kay.

"The rain will go away.

Please stay!" I say.

Bigger raindrops begin to fall. I jump off my swing after Kay.
"This way!" I say.

I lay down my jacket
for us to sit on.

"We can stay dry this way," I tell Kay.

Finally, we see a ray of sunshine. We play tag on our way home.

At home, Mom sets out a tray of milk and cookies. "This is much better," I say. "Will you stay, Kay?"

Word Family: -ay

Word families are groups of words that rhyme and are spelled the same.

Here are the -ay words in this book:

anyway	ray
away	say
day	stay
gray	today
Kay	tray
lay	way
play	

Can you spell any other words with -ay?